"Without leaps of imagination, or dreaming,
we lose the excitement of possibilities."

–GLORIA STEINEM

June 2018

To Yitz, Nevae, and Kayla,
with love.

STERLING CHILDREN'S BOOKS
New York

An Imprint of Sterling Publishing Co., Inc.
1166 Avenue of the Americas
New York, NY 10036

ISBN 978-1-4549-2666-5

Distributed in Canada by Sterling Publishing Co., Inc.
c/o Canadian Manda Group, 664 Annette Street
Toronto, Ontario, M6S 2C8, Canada
Distributed in the United Kingdom by GMC Distribution Services
Castle Place, 166 High Street, Lewes, East Sussex, BN7 1XU, England
Distributed in Australia by NewSouth Books
45 Beach Street, Coogee, NSW 2034, Australia

For information about custom editions, special sales, and premium and
corporate purchases, please contact Sterling Special Sales at 800-805-5489
or specialsales@sterlingpublishing.com.

Manufactured in China

Lot #:
2 4 6 8 10 9 7 5 3 1
12/17

sterlingpublishing.com

Cover and Interior Design by Ryan Thomann
The artwork for this book was created using watercolor, gouache, pencil, and digital media.

Gloria's Voice

The Story of Gloria Steinem—Feminist, Activist, Leader

by AURA LEWIS

STERLING CHILDREN'S BOOKS
New York

This is Gloria. She has big dreams.

She dreams of being famous . . .

. . . and of being a hero who
helps people all over the world.

DINER

Her mama had a dream once, too.
She dreamt of leaving their small town
and doing something big. She dreamt of
being a journalist in New York City.

But as a wife and mother, Gloria's mama has to stay
home and take care of their family. That's what women
are expected to do. That's just the way things are.

Gloria thinks this is very unfair.

When Gloria is ten years old, her parents decide to live in separate homes. They are very different, and their differences make it hard for them to live together.

Gloria misses her papa, who travels far for business.

But the hardest part is when her mama falls ill and can no longer look after Gloria or herself. Sometimes, it's as if Gloria is the grown-up and her mama is the child.

Deep down in her heart of hearts, Gloria wishes her mama had followed her dreams.

Gloria grows up.

She feels ready to leave her small town and do
something big! She dreams of going to New York City.

But first, she wants to travel like her father.
So Gloria journeys across the ocean to India.

She travels with only a sari, a cup, and a comb.
She sees beautiful sights but also a lot of suffering.
There is inequality between the rich and the poor,
and there are wars in the villages.

Gloria joins an aid team that holds meetings for the
villagers. They come and talk about their fears, and Gloria
listens. "Thank you," they say and bring her gifts of rice.
"We never thought anyone from the outside cared." Gloria is
overjoyed knowing that she's making a difference in people's lives.

Arabian Sea

India

After two years in India, Gloria decides it's time
to go to New York City, the land of dreams and
possibilities. Gloria wants to keep helping people,
just as she did in India. She becomes a journalist.
She hopes to report on people and their struggles.

Yet, at the magazines she works for, Gloria is asked to write about hair, beauty products, and . . . stockings!

These are fun but are not the kinds of issues that Gloria is passionate about. Gloria feels like a typewriter without a ribbon.

She realizes that even in New York, the opportunities for women are limited—because the people in charge are all men! They give most of the interesting assignments to other men. They leave little room for a woman's voice.

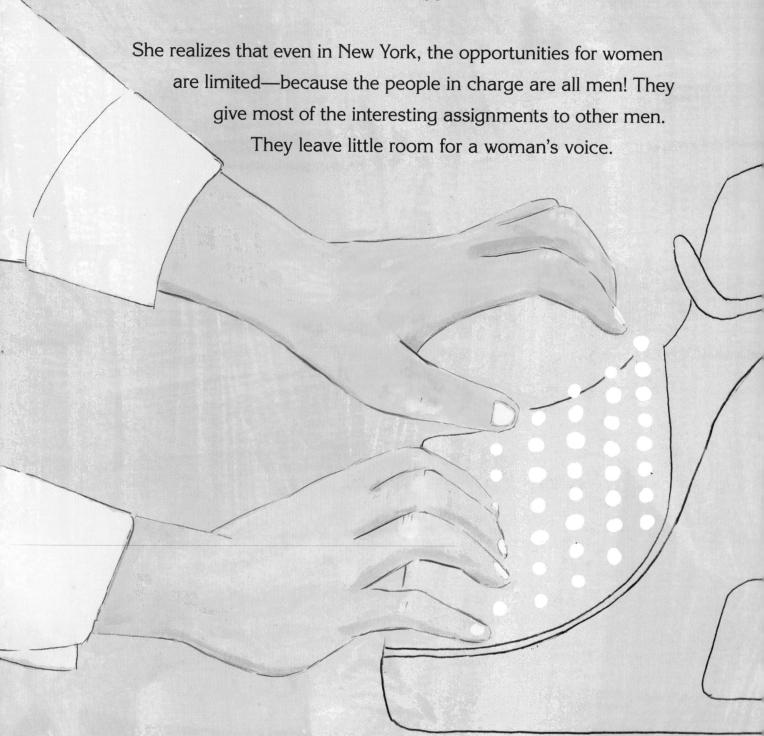

And Gloria wants to be heard.

Gloria is inspired.

She realizes that, just like her, women everywhere want to be heard. And she believes that she can help give them a voice.

Gloria asks her fearless friend Dorothy for help. She hopes that if they speak out for equality together, people will listen. Dorothy can't wait.

The two friends travel all over the country. They give speeches about women's rights. They talk about respecting all people, no matter what they look like or where they come from.

Gloria wants to spread the word even more about feminism and equality.

But how? she wonders.

Then Gloria has a big idea.

To make her idea happen, Gloria
knows that she'll need many people
to come together.

With the help of Dorothy and other
friends, Gloria starts a new kind
of magazine. It's all about women,
and only women are in charge.

They call it *Ms.* magazine.
Ms. magazine gives women a voice.

Gloria is excited to see *Ms.* out in the world,
but she's also scared.

She wonders what people will think. They're
not used to seeing this kind of magazine.
They're not used to women being in charge.

Many news reporters speak out against Gloria's ideas. They predict that the magazine will fail.

But it doesn't. In fact, it is a smash hit. The magazines fly off the newsstands! People want to hear what women have to say.

Gloria is delighted.

The magazine's success gives her hope. Hope that all doors will open to women. Hope that there will be equality between women and men.

"I'm a hope-a-holic!" she says.

Gloria knows there is still a lot of work to do before her hopes become a reality. She has big dreams, and she has only just begun.

Never
Stop
dreaming

Gloria Marie Steinem

was born on March 25, 1934, in Toledo, Ohio, to Ruth and Leo Steinem. Leo, a traveling businessman, often took the family with him on his travels. Gloria and her sister Susanne, nine years her senior, did not attend school during those times. After her parents' divorce in 1944, Gloria lived with her ailing mother until her senior year in high school, when she moved to Washington, D.C., to live with Susanne. She then followed in her sister's footsteps to Smith College in Northampton, MA. After graduating with honors, Gloria spent two years in India on a fellowship before moving to New York City in 1960.

In 1971, she cofounded *Ms.* magazine and became recognized as a leader and media spokesperson for the feminist movement. She has since traveled widely while advocating for women's rights and equality. In 2005, Gloria cofounded the Women's Media Center along with Jane Fonda and Robin Morgan. The Women's Media Center is an organization that "makes women visible and powerful in the media."

Gloria has written many books and has received numerous awards for her writing. One of her well-known books is *Outrageous Acts and Everyday Rebellions*, a collection of essays about women and their struggle for equality. In 2013, she was honored with the Presidential Medal of Freedom for her contribution to women's rights.

Today, Gloria continues to travel internationally as a lecturer and organizer and promotes issues of equality and peace around the world. In addition to her interest in gender and race, Gloria fights against child abuse and advocates for indigenous peoples. When she's not on the road, Gloria lives in New York City.

TO LEARN MORE ABOUT GLORIA,

feminism, and other important women activists,
check out these recommended books.

Ashby, Ruth and Deborah Gore Ohrn, eds. *Herstory: Women Who Changed the World*. New York: Viking Children's Books, 1995.

Chin-Lee, Cynthia. *Amelia to Zora: Twenty-Six Women Who Changed the World*. Watertown, MA: Charlesbridge, 2008.

Dray, Philip. *Yours for Justice, Ida B. Wells: The Daring Life of a Crusading Journalist*. Atlanta: Peachtree Publishers, 2008.

Fabiny, Sarah. *Who is Gloria Steinem?* New York: Grosset & Dunlap, 2014.

Levy, Debbie. *I Dissent: Ruth Bader Ginsburg Makes Her Mark*. New York: Simon & Schuster, 2016.

McDonnell, Patrick. *Me . . . Jane*. New York: Little, Brown Books for Young Readers, 2011.

Parker, Kate T. *Strong Is the New Pretty: A Celebration of Girls Being Themselves*. New York: Workman, 2017.

Schatz, Kate. *Rad American Women A–Z: Rebels, Trailblazers, and Visionaries Who Shaped Our History . . . and Our Future!* San Francisco: City Lights Publishers, 2015.

PAGE-BY-PAGE NOTES

As a child, Gloria read many books and was inspired by the character Jo March in Louisa May Alcott's *Little Women*. Gloria admired Jo for being a writer and having an independent spirit.

Tap dancing is one of Gloria's lifelong passions. She sometimes thought that dancing would get her out of Toledo. Gloria first learned to tap dance from Ruby Brown, a dancer at the resort the Steinems owned during Gloria's childhood.

Gloria loved to read *Wonder Woman* as a child. At that time, Wonder Woman was the first and only female superhero, and Gloria wanted to be just like her. Gloria continues to admire her as an adult for being a hero who uses love and truth to fight for what's right.

Gloria's mother Ruth was a society reporter and Sunday editor at the *Toledo Blade*. She had a secret dream to run away to New York City and work as a journalist.

Gloria adored her father Leo, who treated her as his equal. Their relationship gave Gloria the idea that men and women should be treated the same.
In 1944, Ruth and Leo separated. Ruth, who suffered from mental illness, was prescribed medicine that made it hard to run a household and take care of Gloria and her sister. In many ways, Gloria was in charge. She dreamt of escaping that world.

In 1957, Gloria traveled to India on a fellowship and stayed for two years. She fell in love with India's culture and people, especially with the teachings of Mohandas Gandhi (1869–1948). Gandhi's teachings inspired movements for

freedom all over the world, and Gloria was greatly influenced by them as a feminist leader. She learned that change comes from the people and that in order to learn, you must listen.

Gloria moved to New York City in 1960. She worked as a freelance writer for publications such as *New York Magazine*, *Glamour*, *Harper's Bazaar*, and *Ladies' Home Journal*.

Gloria wanted to write about what was really interesting to her—politics and social issues. She was frustrated to learn that most of the serious news items were covered by male journalists and women were expected to write about fashion, beauty, and home-making.

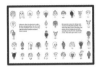 In 1969, Gloria was sent to cover a rally by a radical feminist group called the Redstockings, who spoke out for women's liberation. Gloria, frustrated by society's restrictions on women, realized that their struggle was her own.

Gloria was a reluctant public speaker. She asked her friend Dorothy Pitman Hughes (b. 1938), who founded a daycare center for working mothers, to tour with her and spread the word about feminism and equal rights.

 Gloria and Dorothy cofounded *Ms.* magazine in 1971. It was first published as an insert in *New York* magazine and by 1972 was released separately. It is still being published today.

When *Ms.* magazine was first published, there were many voices who predicted its failure. *The New York Times* called feminism a "passing fad." Harry Reasoner, a well-known television commentator on ABC and CBS News, gave *Ms.* magazine "six months before it ran out of things to say."

 These pages feature several notable people from Gloria's life. Second in line is Gloria's close friend, Wilma Mankiller (1945–2010). Wilma was the first female principal chief of the Cherokee Nation. She served in this role from 1985 to 1995. The two women met when Mankiller joined the board for the Ms. Foundation for Women.

 Third in line is Bella Abzug, who was also known as "Battling Bella" (1920–1998). Bella was an antiwar activist, politician, lawyer, and leader of the women's movement. In 1971, Bella, Gloria, and other leading feminists founded the National Women's Political Caucus.

 The man in the image is David Bale (1941–2003), an entrepreneur, environmentalist, and animal rights activist. Gloria and David were married in 2000 when Gloria was sixty-six years old. They were married for three years before David passed away.

This book offers a small taste of Gloria Steinem's rich life.
To learn more about Gloria, you can begin by visiting her website:
GLORIASTEINEM.COM